The Little Book of the
KAMA SUTRA

or

Camel Sutra

The Little Book of the
KAMA SUTRA

or

Camel Sutra

by

Rohan Candappa

Illustrations by Nick Potter

EBURY PRESS
LONDON

First published in Great Britain in 2002

10 9 8 7 6 5 4 3 2 1

© Rohan Candappa

Illustrations by Nick Potter

First published by
Ebury Press
Random House
20 Vauxhall Bridge Road
London SW1 2SA

Random House Australia (Pty) Limited
20 Alfred Street, Milsons Point, Sydney
New South Wales 2061, Australia

Random House New Zealand Limited
18 Poland Road, Glenfield, Auckland 10, New Zealand

Random House South Africa (Pty) Limited
Endulini, 5A Jubilee Road, Parktown 2193, South Africa

Random House UK Limited Reg. No. 954009
www.randomhouse.co.uk

A CIP catalogue record for this book is available from the British Library
ISBN 0091880688

Papers used by Ebury Press are natural, recyclable products
made from wood grown in sustainable forests

Designed by anizdamani@aol.com
Printed by Nørhaven Paperback A/S, Denmark

For   * who taught me
all I ever needed to know about sex.

And more than I ever needed
to know about   .*

* Please fill in this personalised comedy
dedication as applicable.

1

The Camel Sutra: a Brief History

Camels, for so long celebrated in the west as being no more than ships of the desert, have always harboured within their culture a secret that only now is coming to cast them in an entirely different light. That secret is love. And the practice of love.

Camels are the masters (and mistresses) of the arts and artistries of lovemaking.

At first cud this may seem an absurd notion, but delve deeper and a logic emerges. For a start, there's not a lot to do in a desert. And seeing as camels are somewhat deficient in the hands, fingers and bucket & spade department, it's not as if they could pass the time building sandcastles.

Spend mile after mile, day after day, century after century plodding along through an unchanging and uninteresting landscape and you have to find something to occupy your mind. And what better to think about, ponder on and philosophise over than sex. Especially if your opportunities to indulge in the joys of congress are limited to brief nights of passion on those rare occasions when you encounter a kindred spirit lingering suggestively, at oasis edge.

Given these rather limiting set of romantic circumstances, would not any camel of pluck and vim endeavour to ensure that every chance they have to make love be as blissful and ecstatic as possible? Hence *The Camel Sutra* – the sacred text that centuries ago instructed inexperienced he-camels and she-camels in the ways, means and hoofsteps that lead to both physical and spiritual ecstasy.

I first heard whisper of these legendary texts while working in a small pet emporium just south west of the Hangar Lane gyratory system. Word reached me from a depressed hyacinth macaw who'd heard it from a slow loris who, apparently, had heard it from a three legged armadillo, who in turn had picked up the tale from a commune of itinerant and, frankly, lost alpaca living rough on the outskirts of the ancient city of Thebes.

Despite the garbled nature of the recounting, I was intrigued. Intrigued enough to resign my tenure within said emporium and embark on a quest that would take me deep into uncharted territories both geographically and personally. I am sworn to secrecy as to where I eventually located the texts revealed within, but suffice it to say that I owe a large debt of gratitude to a camel I can only refer to here as 'Kenneth'.

In translating and transcribing *The Camel Sutra* I have endeavoured to be as faithful in spirit and in intent to the original as possible.

The Union of the Cow

In this, classic, position the she-camel stands and lowers her snout as if to graze a tuft of rock pampas, while her he-camel partner raises his forelegs and mounts her from behind, thrusting his lingam deep into her waiting yoni.

This is very much the 'missionary position' of the love-making world of camels. It is where all camels start before studying the tenets of *The Camel Sutra*. For men and women, however, this 'basic' position is somewhat more challenging, especially for the female. They have to stand up, bend over and rest their hands on the ground whilst looking at the floor. For this reason this position is sometimes termed The Union of the Dropped Contact Lens.

The Hyena's Congress

A classic lovemaking position in the world of camels. As the he-camel's fore-hooves are free he is able to caress his partner's withers and hump, and also to stimulate her yoni.

N.B. In a world in which we're all increasingly time poor, and hence make love less often, this position is a godsend as it enables men and women to combine activities e.g. the woman could easily flick through an Argos catalogue while the relatively flat surface afforded by her back makes an ideal resting place for a Pot Noodle or laptop computer.

The Eyes of Love

Another basic position for many camel couples. The he-camel lies atop his recumbent partner, enabling each to look the other in the eyes.

(Popular at the start of man–woman relationships, this position tends to fall from favour as time passes and looking your partner in the eye during the horizontal rumba is the last thing you want to do.)

The Folded Position

In this position the she-camel folds herself up like a freshly pressed yashmak.

Only comfortably achievable by those of exceptionally loose limbs, morals and clothing.

The Lotus Position

In this position the he-camel sits cross-legged on the sands of the desert and the she-camel sits on his lap, snout to snout with him and lowers her yoni onto his lingam.

Please note in this position the female bears the responsibility for the supply of friction generating activity. The male can do little more than initiate rather comical little bouncing motions. However he can sneakily switch on the TV with the remote control and watch the second half of the Champions' League match without his partner knowing, as long as he keeps the volume turned down, and times his orgasm to coincide with his team scoring.

The Congress of the Splitting Fig

Camels are phenomenally skilled at oral sex. After all, it's not just by accident that they have such mobile lips and such long, muscular tongues.

The Yawning Position

In this position the he-camel is on top and the she-camel underneath. While the he-camel is ensconced within his partner's yoni she raises her rear legs and parts them widely.

In my researches on sexuality in the west I have discovered that most women have experienced a vast range of yawning positions in their love-making. However 'yawning' in these cases often has an entirely different meaning.

The Collapsed Yawning Position

From the embraces of The Yawning Position it is but a short slip of the fetlock to The Collapsed Yawning Position in which the splayed nature of the she-camel's rear legs allows the he-camel to press the plough that is his lingam deep into the furrow that is her yoni.

In the west this position is sometimes referred to as The Bicycle Rack and has the added benefit for the female, as well as great satisfaction due to the depth of penetration, of affording the surreptitious opportunity to check whether one's toenails need re-varnishing.

The Dune Top

In this position the she-camel supports her belly and brisket on the crest of a dune or other handily placed surface.

N.B. If you don't have easy access to a dune top then a kitchen table, office desk or the lid of one of the freezer cabinets at a larger Kwik Save supermarket will do.

The Felled Palm Tree

In this position the he and she-camel lie alongside each other with their rear legs outstretched. The she-camel raises one leg slightly to allow the he-camel to enter, then he raises his leg and rests it on hers.

A good position for men who enjoy extra friction during intercourse. Of course, there are many other ways of increasing friction during sex, but steer clear of any technique involving the use of sandpaper or velcro.

Launching the Felucca

I recommend this position for couples where the female partner speaks constantly during lovemaking with a really irritating voice. Or the male partner suffers from particularly cold ears.

The Suspended Congress

In this position the he-camel leans against a handily located palm tree as the she-camel puts her fore-legs around his neck while he lifts her up by locking his hooves under her flanks and she wraps her hind legs around him and exerts leverage on his lingam with her yoni by pushing her hooves against the palm tree.

Rarely attempted by the heftier camels in a herd.

The Toppled Goat

For the she-camel this position is not the easiest to maintain for any length of time. However it is recommended for the he-camel with a shorter lingam. (And the she-camel with a shorter attention span.)

The Gaping Position

In this deeply satisfying position mounds of sands or coconut husks are used to support and arch the lower back of the she-camel. As a result the opening of the yoni is pushed up firmly to meet and greet the oncoming thrusts of the incoming lingam.

(N.B. Well loved by she-camels everywhere this position is thought to be the origin of the old camelic proverb, 'From gaping to gasping takes but a little grasping'.)

The Milk and Water Embrace

In the Milk and Water Embrace the she-camel lies alongside the he-camel and wraps all four legs around him and pulls him deep within. It is one of the most sensuous positions within The Camel Sutra and represents total acceptance by each partner of the other.

In the west I have been experimenting with what I term the Cheese and Pickle Embrace which is very similar, if somewhat more sandwich-like and crunchy, in the arrangement of the limbs.

Chewing the Sphinx's Nose

Camels aren't only experts at oral stimulation, but they also enjoy it so much that they indulge at every opportunity. (Which kind of explains the spitting thing.)

The Top

**A most advanced and dexterity demand-
ing position. At first glance the she-camel
appears to be doing little more than sitting
astride the he-camel. But to achieve this
congress successfully she must achieve the
position illustrated and then rotate upon
his lingam.**

An awkward and tricky position that, in truth,
provides little pleasure. However it is a useful
way for the female partner to scan the room for
light snacks, dropped earrings and hidden
agendas.

The Snake Trap

To complete The Snake Trap the she-camel sits astride the he-camel, facing him, and each holds the other just above the hooves. The he and she-camel then rock back and forward, simulating the motion of a dhow rising and falling on the currents of the Nile.

Frankly this position is more effort than it is worth. I would suggest that you only attempt it if you are either bored, drunk or need to discuss with your partner what to cook for when your parents come round for lunch on Sunday.

The Turning Position

Ideal for camels who've fallen out over a minor dispute but still fancy a bit of the old how's your felucca. (Or camels with a serious hoof fetish thing going on.)

The Crab's Position

This position has long been popular with coastal dwelling camels. The she-camel lies down facing her partner then raises and draws in both legs, resting her hocks on his stomach in a manner which resembles a crab retracting its claws.

This position can often evolve into The Lobster's Position which is similar, if somewhat more elongated. Skilled practitioners of *The Camel Sutra* may then attempt The Scampi's Position which involves both partners being lightly coated in breadcrumbs prior to love-making.

The Swinging Mane

Popular with she-camels with long, fabulous manes, this position allows them to toss their hair wantonly from side to side, with great abandon, when the heights of sexual ecstasy come within clambering distance.

(With the male and female positions reversed this is, apparently, a great favourite with Mr D Ginola.)

The Sky at Night

The prone she-camel rests her rear fetlocks either side of her kneeling partner's neck while he introduces his lingam into her yoni. (A brief introduction is best, with few formalities.) By pressing her quarters and stifles together she squeezes his lingam, increasing the friction – and hence the sensations, that both experience.

It is important not to squeeze too tightly as the female's ankles can easily cut off the blood supply to the males head, rendering him unconscious. This leaves the female stuck in what is often termed the 'My Word, It Really Is About Time We Re-Papered the Ceiling Position'.

The Twining Position

In this position the he-camel lies atop the prone she-camel who places one fetlock across her partner's rump and pulls him towards her.

Please make sure not to confuse this position with The Twinings Position in which both partners attempt a similar juxtaposition whilst imbibing cups of lukewarm Lapsang Souchong tea.

The Elephant Posture

The she-camel lies upon the sands of the desert. The he-camel lies on top of her and arches his back upwards. Rhythmic clasping and unclasping also heightens the sensations.

If the male partner in a couple is, – how can I most delicately put this? – somewhat less than svelte, it will soon become apparent to the female partner why this position is termed The Elephant Posture.

The Camel's Wheel

The he-camel sits with his fetlocks out-stretched and parted, his partner lowers herself onto his lingam, extending her quarters over the side of his flanks. Thus the he-camel, in congress with the she-camel, creates the spokes of a metaphorical and, indeed, metaphysical wheel.

A most enjoyable conjunction just as long as you ensure that the 'hub' of this particular 'wheel' is sufficiently 'greased' before inserting the 'axle'. (Very popular with Kwik Fit fiters.)

The Scarf

In this suppleness-demanding conjunction the she-camel starts with one leg over her partner's withers, then lowers that leg and raises the other one.

This position is recommended only for the young, drunk or, ideally, the young and drunk. However it is, apparently, popular among female hurdlers in pre-Olympic training.

The Paired Hooves

Only for the gullible. (Sometimes referred to as The Position of the Now What?).

The Twisted Eel

The he-camel and she-camel lie invertedly recumbent. The head of each points to the fore-hooves of the other, allowing mutual simultaneous snouto-genital stimulation to occur. Deep bliss often results.

Be warned that in vigorous lovemaking sessions The Twisted Eel often melds seamlessly into the rather louche position known as The Thrashing Halibut. On no account, however, let your passions drive you on to The Giddy Kipper. That way madness lies.

Love Signs of the Camel Sutra

Spend an eternity plodding across the vast featureless expanses of the desert, using little more than the position of the stars to navigate by and you will, inevitably, pass much time considering said stars. Their positions. Their juxtapositions. And their influence on your life.

Camelstrology is an ancient and complex subject. Many a learned and lengthy tome have been devoted to it and even they but skim the surface of the deep well of wisdom that exists within the minds of the much revered Astrologer Camels of the Kalahari.

In Love Signs of *The Camel Sutra* I have interpreted camelstrology into the sphere of love and love-making and applied it to the situation of the man and woman today. You will find it an invaluable tool in helping you discover your, and your partner's, cosmic nature as a lover.

The Signs of Camelstrology

Mosquito	January 27–February 15
Palm Tree	February 16–March 11
Pyramids	March 12–April 23
Hyena	April 24–May 20
Gecko	May 21–June 4
Dung Beetle	June 5–July 31
Cactus	August 1–August 30
Mirage	August 31–September 19
Yashmaks	September 20–October 15
Oasis	October 16–November 22
Scorpion	November 23–December 15
Vultures	December 16–January 25

The Mosquito
(January 27–February 15)

Mosquitoes make the most annoying of lovers. They just don't seem to be able to settle on a single course of action. They start nibbling one part of your body and just as it's beginning to turn you on, they're up and off to another part. And the same thing happens there. They also tend to make a lot of noise when making love. Unfortunately, as the noise they make is little more than a high-pitched whine, it is far from seductive or arousing.

In their favour, Mosquitoes are very persistent lovers and can keep up their performance all night, especially if the weather is warm. They also enjoy mild corporal punishment and much fun can be had chasing them naked round the bedroom with a paperback or rolled-up magazine.

The Palm Tree
(February 16–March 11)

As lovers Palm Trees are somewhat unanimated. Some experts have even described them as 'wooden'. Even in the throes of the most earth-shattering orgasm they will do little more than just 'sway' a little. They also tend to steer clear of sexual positions that involve much, or indeed any, movement.

At a party, any individual you observe rooted to the spot, not circulating at all, or talking much, is likely to be a Palm Tree. Palm Trees also tend to suffer from very rough skin. On the other hand, male Palm Trees have erections that last all night and massive nuts.

The Pyramid
(March 12–April 23)

Everything about a Pyramid is larger than life. Their personality is a big personality that shouts out 'look at me, look at me'. And you do. Go to bed with a Pyramid and the experience will be much the same. You will inevitably feel impressed by the sheer scale of what, sexually, is on offer to you. In many ways it can be a little daunting.

Unfortunately when you get closer to the action you will soon discover that making love to a Pyramid can be very hard work. And impressive though they no doubt are, you can easily end up wondering if it was really worth the effort.

The Hyena
(April 24–May 20)

Hyenas are the life and soul of the party. They're always in the thick of things and they've always got a smile on their face and a quip up their sleeve. They tend to have no trouble finding partners as they benefit from the current, in my opinion misguided, notion that a good sense of humour is very sexy.

Unfortunately should you take this 'life and soul of the party' back to your place after the party you'll soon discover that they go on being the life and soul even when the party just comprises the two of you. Hyenas laugh at everything, which can be very disconcerting as you're getting undressed.

The Gecko

(May 21–June 4)

Geckos make incredibly agile and adventurous lovers. They'll try anything and go anywhere to make love. For them a bed is just for sleeping. They'll venture on tables, under tables, against walls, up trees, even against mirrors and windows to bonk.

For these reasons after a typical love-making session with a Gecko you may well have to be scraped off the ceiling. And you won't believe the things they can do with those long tongues of theirs. On the down side they do tend to have large protruding eyes and enjoy eating flies.

The Dung Beetle

(June 5–July 31)

Dung Beetles are anally retentive both as people and as lovers. For them everything has a place and everything should be in its place. And until it is they probably can't relax and definitely can't enjoy sex. If you've ever made love to someone who first folded all their clothes and arranged them into a shop-worthy display before getting into bed with you then, mid thrust, leapt up and out of the bed screaming 'Oh my God I've left the milk out of the fridge' – they were probably a Dung Beetle.

For this and many, many other reasons Dung Beetles experience few orgasms. Instead they roll up often years of unfulfilled orgasmic energy into a massive ball of frustration and fury. Having said all that if you're the person that they're with when that ball finally breaks open then you're in for a hell of a night.

The Cacti

(August 1–August 30)

Cacti, in every day life, are notoriously difficult people to approach. Likewise in all matters related to love. Everything about their attitude and demeanour shrieks out 'Keep Away'. They believe that everyone else in the world is out to hurt them, so live the maxim that 'the best form of defence is attack'.

In matters of love and sexuality this means that a typical Cactus will dress themselves up in an aura of aggression and threat. That's why if you're a Cactus you're probably into leather, bondage and other fetishistic lifestyles. However, beneath the spiky exterior most Cacti are really soft, succulent and gorgeously fleshy.

The Mirage
(August 31–September 19)

Mirages are hard to pin down in life. And in bed. They appear to be the most wonderful of people with everything going for them, but when you get close to them everything that was appealing seems to vanish into thin air. Many politicians are Mirages.

In bed they can be just as frustrating as in other areas. Breasts that appear to be too good to be true, turn out to be just that. Lingams that look a promising size in repose turn out actually to shrink when aroused. And love-making that was heralded to stretch long into the early hours, ends so abruptly that you don't even reach foreplay and falter somewhere around twoplay.

The Yashmak
(September 20–October 15)

Yashmaks are often assumed to be shy and retiring, both in life and in bed. Nothing could be further from the truth. The outer, demure appearance of the Yashmak, in fact, masks an interior that is pure passion. How to get past the exterior is, however, something that has perplexed and confounded countless frustrated suitors over the centuries. The answer lies in the old camelic proverb that 'Some doors open only from the inside'.

When it comes to love-making Yashmaks tend to thrash about, scream out quite detailed obscenities and reach, at regular intervals, for bedside cabinets that discretely bulge with a startling selection of accoutrements.

The Oasis

(October 16–November 22)

An Oasis is the most welcoming person you could hope to meet. They'll put you at your ease. They'll soak away all your troubles and cares. And you'll leave their company feeling refreshed and revived. At parties and in life people congregate around an Oasis to bask in their generosity and bonhomie. And therein lies the flaw in the otherwise perfect diamond that is an Oasis.

You will never have an Oasis exclusively to yourself. And frustrating though this can be in the day-to-day life of a relationship, it's even worse when you arrive at the bedchamber. There you'll be luxuriating seductively in the welcoming arms, legs and everything else of your Oasis partner, when a knock will come on the door and before you know it the bedroom will look like that scene in the ship's cabin in that Marx Brothers movie.

The Scorpion

(November 23–December 15)

Scorpions as lovers are taut, honed and gleaming. And once in their embrace, it's hard to escape. Everything they do has an air of excitement and danger. Go to bed with a Scorpion and you can expect to be tied up, slavered in WD 40, and forced to rip off a leather thong with your bare teeth.

But do the wrong thing and it can all be over in an instant. And Scorpions do also have the rather unappealing habit of scurrying about when they move, and lurking in gloomy corners or crevices when they don't.

Incidentally, they make cracking flamenco dancers.

The Vulture

(December 16–January 25)

The Vulture is probably the most unappealing of all signs in Camelstrology. There is very little that's good to be said about them either as people or lovers.

They tend to order ribs in restaurants.

N.B. The astute amongst you may have noticed that the Camel Zodiac fails to cover anyone born on the 26th of January. No satisfactory explanation has ever been given for this.

How to Drive Your He-Camel Wild In the Dunes

This part of *The Camel Sutra*, with its short hints and suggestions, and somewhat 'in your face' title was added to the original, more contemplative texts, comparatively recently. Many of the more conservative scholars of the arts of camel love frown upon their 'quick-fix' nature. I, on the other hand, believe them to be an invaluable aid in a modern age where we are all increasingly time poor. Hence I include these lust-inducing suggestions for your perusal.

The She-Camel that Feels Sexy Is Sexy

Great sex starts in the head. In your head. Think of yourself as gorgeous. Picture your flanks as taut, your fetlocks as enticing and your humps as pert.

A Self-Confident She-Camel Is a Sex Confident She-Camel

A camel that's got confidence can get what she wants. So walk the walk, and talk the talk.

Focus on Him and He'll Focus on You.

Make your he-camel feel like the only he-camel in the Sahara and you'll soon have him eating out of your hoof.

'Is That a Palm Tree Under Your Saddle, or Are You Just Happy to See Me?'

The average he-camel can be a little bit backward in coming forward. So tell him that you want him. There's no greater turn on for a he-camel than being desired.

Don't Whisper Sweet Nothings

While she-camels can respond to gentle, romantic muses nuzzled from their partners muzzles, he-camels would rather cut straight to the chase. In brief, talk dirty to him. Tell him what you'd like to do to him down in the dunes, and what you'd like him to do to you. Be specific. Very specific.

Reflections of Love

Before making love just happen to position your-self by the waterhole of an oasis.

Few he-camels can resist the added excitement of seeing themselves mounting their partner's croup.

Make Love in Unusual Places

Don't restrict yourself to the dunes. Try perching on the edge of a well. Or leaning against a palm tree. Or round the back of a pyramid. Or even in a quiet corner of the casbah.

Surprise Him at Work

There he is, plodding along the same old track, carrying yet another fat, bored tourist on his back, then he rounds a corner and finds you, standing with your rump flexing seductively and your muzzle dripping. Who wouldn't be turned on?

Put on a Fashion Show

Find the skimpiest, tightest, sexiest saddle you can then parade up and down in front of him. For added arousal tell him he can look but can't touch.

The Love that Binds

Get him to tether you to a palm tree and take his pleasure with you. Then do the same to him.

Visit the Sunset Strip

As the sun sets behind you, remove your harness, saddle and bits as slowly and seductively as you can. For added arousal, when you're down to the very last part of your tack, get your partner to remove it from your panting body using only his teeth and his tongue.

Out of Sight, Out of His Mind

Put blinkers on your he-camel before you make love to him. The extra vulnerability he'll feel will just add to the eroticism of what is to come.

A Real Flight of Fantasy

Feathers can be a most erotic love toy. They can brush, or tickle, or scratch. Especially sensitive to the touch of a feather are the snout, brisket, withers, lingam and scrotum. And why stop at just one feather? Really adventurous she-camels might like to try using the whole chicken.

Fruit Bowl Him Over

Let's just say that there's more than one box you can eat a fig from...

Tell It Like It Is

While making love to your he-camel, tell him
how good it feels. For example,

'Oh baby, you're as hard as a pyramid'
'You're making my oasis overflow'
'Fetlock me'
'Fetlock me harder'

An Apology

The advice in the preceding section concerns itself solely with hints to the she-camel as to how to pleasure her he-camel. Legend has it that the she-camel that penned this advice was about to embark on a tome guiding he-camels in the arts of pleasuring she-camels when she split up, rather acrimoniously, from her partner.

Hence when she attempted to write this second missive she got no further that the somewhat bitter title 'How To Stop Your She-Camel Nodding Off While You Spend Ages Rummaging Around Trying To Find Her Gee-Gee Spot'.

(N.B. The Gee-Gee spot is, apparently, a location within the she-camel's yoni that if found and stimulated is suppose to have even the most matronly of she-camels thrashing about like a frisky young filly.)

4

The Amorata Camela

(The Love Poems of The Camel Sutra)

From the fifteenth century onwards all surviving examples of *The Camel Sutra* have included the suite of love poems that have come to be known as The Amorata Camela.

The Amorata Camela tells over the course of ten poems of the romance between a young he-camel F'taa and his love F'qaa. The actual identity of the lovers has never been satisfactorily established but many scholars believe F'taa to have been a prince of Saharan extraction and F'qaa a servant she-camel from what is now the Saudi Arabian peninsula.

For obvious reasons such a love affair between a he-camel of royal blood and a she-camel of far humbler origins would have been taboo. However many see this as only adding to the romanticism of the whole affair and increasing the heart-rending pathos of the final denouement.

Whatever the truth that lies behind The Amorata Camela it is love poetry of the highest order that cannot fail to move the heart, stir the loins and moisten even the most cynical eye.

Indeed recite extracts from The Amorata Camela to your love at apposite moments in your relationship and they will find it almost impossible to resist.

First Encounter

One sight

of your magnificent

withers

and I was

lost

One glance

through your eyelashes

as long as

The Mother Nile

and I was

found

Pursuit

From the emerald hued waters
of Wadi al Jaffir
Aboudi
to the low lying
bluffs
of the early
stages
of the Atlas
mountains
and their immediate environs
my caravanserai
will not rest
till you and I
unite
unencumbered

Flirtation

Your humps

are pert

my love

How sweetly

they oscillate

when ever

you

trot

Seduction

Let me
strum
your zither
with my fetlock
Let me
play melodies of loving
on the
taut drum skin
of your rear hind quarters
Till you fall
sated
among the
cabbage palm foliage

Acquiescence

You

offer me

your juicy grape

ripe for plucking

My tender stem

of asparagus

hardens

Consummation

Bending low

you sip

the crystal clear waters

of desire

while I

fill you up

more than once

from the rear

with

my solidified

passion

Conflagration

Sand

gets

everywhere

when

we meet

as

one

It chafes!

It chafes!

It is

the chafing

of love

Afterglow

Depleted

I slip

from your

oasis

My snout

nuzzling your

withers

as your humps

heave

with diminishing

intensity

Parting

All

flowers

wilt

All

fruit

fall

All

paths

diverge

In

time

Regret

Marrakech!

Marrakech!

Don't say

Marrakech!

The memories

are too

bitter

The memories

are too

sweet

5

Tantric Sex

I would be remiss to bring you the wisdom of *The Camel Sutra* without mentioning tantric sex. The word 'tan' means expansion and 'tra' translates as tool. Hence tantric sex is sex that is utilised as a tool for expansion on physical, psychological and spiritual levels. It is an expedition into a realm of the senses where sex and sexuality are paths to a harmonization of life energies and a resolution of contradictions and conflicts in order to experience life as a flow of intense energy.

And, according to Sting, it helps you bonk continuously for seven hours at a stretch without even needing a break for a cup of tea or a bag of pork scratchings.

There is, of course, a yin to the yang of tantric sex that has long been practised by the camels of this world. And it is a subject upon which, until now, hardly anything has been written. I speak, of course, of *Tantrum Sex*.

Tantrum Sex

I was first alerted to the existence of Tantrum Sex by Herbie Cous-Cous, one time lead marimba player of the sixties free jazz group The Fancy Cheese People. Herbie, who now runs a consciousness-raising bakery in Antibes, puts the attractions of Tantrum Sex very succinctly in the following statement.

'It's like when you're really pissed off, man, and you resolve all the tension with a short, sharp, shag. And it's over really quickly so you can get all that squelchy business easily sorted in, like, the break for ads during Corrie.'

What follows is some of the wisdom I gleaned at Herbie's feet.

Ten Top Tips for Tip Top Tantrum Sex

1

Forget your partner's birthday.

Ten Top Tips for Tip Top Tantrum Sex

2

Forget your partner's name.

Ten Top Tips for Tip Top Tantrum Sex

3

Call out an ex-lovers name
during foreplay.

Ten Top Tips for Tip Top Tantrum Sex

4

Call an ex-lover's mobile during consumation.

Ten Top Tips for Tip Top Tantrum Sex

5

Bottle up resentment over some minor disagreement, refuse to talk about it all day even when your partner asks you 'what's wrong?' because they 'shouldn't have to ask' and 'if they really loved you they would know what was wrong anyway', then go to bed with them.

Ten Top Tips for Tip Top Tantrum Sex

6

When out for a meal with friends, subtly make fun of your partner.

Ten Top Tips for Tip Top Tantrum Sex

7

Just as your partner commences foreplay, ask them if they could speed it up a tad as there's a repeat of a *Bergerac* on that you don't want to miss.

Ten Top Tips for Tip Top Tantrum Sex

8

During an evening out with your partner's friends, make it obvious that you don't like them.

Ten Top Tips for Tip Top Tantrum Sex

9

During an evening out with your partner's friends, make it obvious that you fancy one of them.

Ten Top Tips for Tip Top Tantrum Sex

10

Half way through love-making casually mention the fact that this isn't the way your last lover used to do it.

Some Other Sutras You Might Be Interested In

In my researches into the profound teachings and ecstatic techniques of *The Camel Sutra* I have come across a myriad of other sutras. Though none have the historic significance, nor encompass the spiritual enlightenment of *The Camel Sutra* they are, to a lesser or greater extent, worth consideration.

After all was it not the Great She-Camel herself who said when returning from her trek of forty days and forty nights across the Plains Of Remorse, 'There are many paths across the wilderness, my brethren'.

The Korma Sutra

In many ways this is the sutra most likely to find favour with a mass audience in the west. It is a mildly exotic collection of sexual positions that while it excites the palette of individuals raised on bland English love making fare, contains nothing too challenging or spicy. Hence if your partner is at all reluctant about diving into the whole sutra business, then The Korma Sutra is a good, creamy, place to start.

The Calmer Sutra

This comprises a series of not very strenuous at all sexual congresses that require little effort and only a modicum of pushing and shoving work. Positions include The Loris, The Slow Loris, and The Slow Loris Who's Had Quite a Big Sunday Lunch.

The Charmer Sutra

This comprises a selection of suavely sophisticated sexual conjugations of a decidedly caddish complexion. For most of the positions described in The Charmer Sutra champagne, black silk sheets and baby oil are de rigeur.

The Cava Sutra

In many ways similar to The Charmer Sutra. However The Cava Sutra is somewhat lower budget in nature. Hence exponents of its arts favour sparkling wine instead of champagne, off-white viscose sheets instead of black silk, and lard instead of baby oil.

The Coma Sutra

Similar to The Calmer Sutra in many ways. The key difference is that the positions described within it involve absolutely no expenditure of energy.

Ideal for couples with babies or young children.

The Como Sutra

Primarily for lovers who like to be sere-
naded with a CD of Easy Listening
classics whilst making 'the camel with
four humps'. It is, in many ways, aural sex
at its finest. Matt Munro, Andy Williams
and the blessed Perry C are the ideal
stereophonic backdrops to your quest for
'magic moments'.

To experience fully the ecstasy achievable
whilst pursuing the tenets of The Como
Sutra, the wearing of patterned sweaters
is recommended, though not compulsory.

The Guava Sutra

These comprise a series of teachings and techniques first laid down by the eminent Scottish warrior-philosopher-greengrocer Cad Boll. This semi-legendary Victorian explorer travelled far and wide collecting exotic fruits from all parts of the globe and experimenting with their sexual possibilities. Guavas, paw-paws, mangosteens and the aptly named kumquats provided the most satisfying revelations.

My only note of caution for those attempting to experience the delights of The Guava Sutra is watch out for the pips.

The Che Guevera Sutra

Very popular in the late 1960s and early 1970s, especially among students, the revolutionary teachings of The Che Guevera Sutra have become little more than a fashion item today. Hence modern-day devotees believe that true sexual freedom and emancipation can be achieved by little more than bearded bonking in berets while listening to a CD of The Buena Vista Social Club.

The Llama Sutra

An exposition of sexual positions to be attempted in high mountainous terrains while wearing large, shaggy overcoats.

The Dalai Llama Sutra

Similar to The Llama Sutra but far, far more spiritual. Usually only attempted by those living in exile. Or Slough.

Apparently Richard Gere is a keen devotee.

The Saga Sutra

A manual of surprisingly raunchy sexual positions only open to the over 55s on holiday in large groups.

The Farmer Sutra

Probably the only series of sexual positions inspired by *The Archers*. Under the tenets of The Farmer Sutra the sexual act is permitted only on weekdays during the sacred fifteen minutes between 7pm and 7.15pm. But may be repeated the next day between 2pm and 2.15pm. No sex is allowed on Saturdays, but on Sunday mornings, however, it is compulsory to repeat all the week's sexual exploits between 10am and 11.15am.

Positions include The Shula, Walter Gabriel's Embrace and The Congress of the Grundys.

The Judith Chalmers Sutra

A manual of somewhat conservative and slightly over-tanned sexual congresses designed to be attempted poolside at luxury hotels in exotic holiday locations or while on excursions to sample the local cuisine and culture.